RAPTURE

Winner of the Walt Whitman Award
of the Academy of American Poets

2015

Selected by Tracy K. Smith

Sponsored by the Academy of American Poets,
the Walt Whitman Award is given annually to the winner
of an open competition among American poets
who have not yet published a book of poems.

RAPTURE

—Poems—

Sjohnna McCray

Graywolf Press

This publication is made possible, in part, by the voters of Minnesota through a Minnesota State Arts Board Operating Support grant, thanks to a legislative appropriation from the arts and cultural heritage fund, and through grants from the National Endowment for the Arts and the Wells Fargo Foundation Minnesota. Significant support has also been provided by Target, the McKnight Foundation, Amazon.com, and other generous contributions from foundations, corporations, and individuals. To these organizations and individuals we offer our heartfelt thanks.

Published by Graywolf Press
250 Third Avenue North, Suite 600
Minneapolis, Minnesota 55401

www.graywolfpress.org

Published in the United States of America

ISBN 978-1-55597-737-5

2 4 6 8 9 7 5 3 1
First Graywolf Printing, 2016

Library of Congress Control Number: 2015953596

Cover design: Kapo Ng

For my mother and father.

For Reetika Vazirani.

For Michael, always.

Contents

Coming Home

My little boy pulls at my coat
as if he's asking me

why did you take so long
to get back home?

Who did you fight with
all those months and years

to win that prize
of snow white hair?

—Tu Mu

RAPTURE

Father & Son by Window

You sing, soft winds & blue seat.

Of course you get the lyrics wrong.
    Dinah sings, soft winds & blue sea.

Dinah will wait near shore for him.
    Father on his chair

underneath the shower's spray.
    Tonight, you flip the night

as if it were a card.
    You scrub his back,

move briskly through the arms.
    You match the constellations

each to a different longing.
    So light you're hefting nothing.

A black square, then another.
    You take the rag to the blunt nose,

over the lips, almost yours.
    By now, the stars are embers,

the numbers are forgotten.
    You follow the knots, the dark scars

on a face turned away from water.
    His memory flickers on —

a light from a porch nearby.

How to Move

I cannot look at anything
    so black as my father's leg
        or used-to-be-leg below the knee,

now a stump. If a child's doll lost
    its flexible hand, the surface
        underneath would be as round

as father's stump. I've touched it once.
    And my brother, who is five,
        is not afraid to touch the stump.

Men on the corner used to holler
    that dad was a high yellow nigger
        or if the sun had darkened him

and pulled the red to the surface of his skin,
    a red nigger. I am thinking of colors
        because the prosthesis comes in colors.

His first leg was the color of oatmeal,
    maybe the color of peaches. Khaki,
        yellow and pink: a simulated sunset.

I am thinking of technicians
    with photographs creating
        perfect shades of negroness

for limbless negroes, every negro
    matched to a swatch or chart with names
        like fingernail polish. When my brother

touches the stump, the stump
　　　　that has shrunk and hardened to look
　　　　　　like an oversized, uncircumcised penis,

when my brother takes the brown
　　　　almost black debris of father's life
　　　　　　into small hands that marvel

at catching spiders in jars, he is not afraid.
　　　　When we discover death, shaking
　　　　　　in the gravel driveway, he knows it

immediately, the dark gray body
　　　　of the robin, the red and slightly pink
　　　　　　shaggy belly. The fuzz of the robin's round belly

like the fuzz of new tennis balls.
　　　　The robin is on its side with the right wing
　　　　　　moving slowly, back and forth.

At the same time, the beak is opening
　　　　and closing. There's hardly any sound, no song
　　　　　　except the sound of short, jagged gasps. All

elements working in unison: wing
　　　　moving back and forth, beak
　　　　　　opening and closing, the rhythm inherent

in knowing and not knowing when anything
　　　　is coming, but wanting to finish it, gracefully.
　　　　　　Even while dying. But maybe grace

has nothing to do with it; maybe
    it's desire that pulls our limbs, the robin's
        wing on concrete, to fly even in the shadow

of a man and a boy, the boy with his eyes
    out of his mind, celestial. Maybe
        the desire is to show us how to move.

When we are at home,
    my brother takes the stump in his arms
        holds on to it like a prize or an unexpected gift

        that father has given us.

Winter Anesthesia

—Veterans Hospital, 1992

It's something like the ache of a missing leg,

    the twitch of an invisible limb.

Like winter in the hills

    when the sleet and snow are so heavy

outside there's only white on white.

    Something happens, no ears.

Head blind with a heart out wild

    in the snow. A cry for a handful of tokens,

a wish for a day without expense,

    an extravagance of small pauses,

many caesuras.

Bedtime Story #1

—Seoul, Korea, 1971

Father gave her a little extra. How could she not

    fall for him? He was handsome

but still a boy. In the depot where soldiers

    took such women, his skinny body clung

too close to hers and his narrow ass still

    belonged to his mother. The other men

knew the routine and how much to pay.

    She loathed their accent and American swagger.

The sweat would barely cool and dry

    before another shook the cot and bucked his hips

out of rhythm—in some other time zone.

    However, he began to offer other things

besides money. He brought sweets from the base

    and the minute he touched his pocket

the face she reserved for his English crumbled

like sweet toffee. Because he didn't know how

to say what he wanted to say, no time

was spent on uneasiness. Chocolate,

caramel and peanuts spoke best, secured

his place. He hooked his arms through hers as if

they could stroll the lane like an ordinary couple:

the unassuming black and the Korean whore

in the middle of the Vietnam War.

His Face Is as Far Away as the Light

His face is as far away as the light
of a farmhouse across dark fields.
The man across from me on the bus
smells. Seven hours or more,
the ride's been all bad weather,
moonless and sober.
His dark skin, titian, hardens to umbra
about the knuckles and the eyes.
He leans toward the window. I think
grief must be circular, the way a man
can hit his head on the silver handle,
awaken, turn, and nod off again.

Comfort Woman

—Seoul, Korea, 1971

This is something my mother knew: to fuck
a man without a metaphor, without

    even the slightest hint of a story,
    is to be at the center of two deaths.

        To see with her eyes is to see as
        a camera lens stripped of gauze:

            the unwelcome influx of light
            reducing men to texture:

                the prickly hairs, the moles and bumps,
                the scarred trenches along the shoulders.

                    Each pause is a wish for things unsaid.
                    The bedsprings in their frailty squeak:

                    Thank God, you whore, thank God.

Neckbone

She is a woman who ties scarves quickly
as an afterthought. So many slashes of silk
hang loose like tongues
waiting to be chosen.
Forlorn until such an occasion
calls for the hint of cinnamon, paprika,
or simply requires black licorice.

At home, she wears mascara
claiming hips that belong
to brassier types, *old* wartime pinups:
Rita Hayworth on the cover of *Life*.
She ties scarves around her waist,
chiffon that whispers
untie me, unravel.

At best, she is a revisionist.
A woman whose country leaves her
with only scarves. Her knots
are a small motif, a closed-up rose,
that shakes with every swallow.

Yellow Apples

She brings yellow apples and stands
outside the motel in the same lime dress
he's seen her in the last six times.

Cinched at the waist and modestly cut.
And if she stands perfectly still, maybe
he'll overlook her cheap, black flats

where the outline of each toe
makes her vulnerable. Even done up
with her hair curled. It's late evening,

a mild breeze runs down the hill
and moonlight falls on her crumpled bag,
which sags a little from the apples. For a moment,

she forgets why she's standing there:
diaphragm and condoms in her purse.

Smoke & Mirrors

This surprises Persephone: weariness,
a face she wore as a youth, peels away
as she matures. Her body demands
less light & her skin feels porcelain smooth
in the soot of Hades' hands. There is
comfort in the old man's arms. As a child,
she hid among her mother's skirts. The cool silks
raised the hair on her arms much the same way
he does when pulling her close & swapping
the air from her lungs with the smoke on
his breath. She'll have to explain to her mother
the excavation of her heart
along with breasts & hips. No longer the shy girl,
she relishes both lives: above & below.

Postcard: Turning Stations

—Cincinnati, Ohio, 1972

Dear Sister,

America.

Late nights, we lie under the spread and listen
to the stereo jazz sounds of WTKO
on the FM station. He says I am so fine
in my tight, pulled-back and strapless
bed-sheet gown. Imagine, the polyester
with sequins. A sultry Dinah Washington.

Turn.   He puts a pillow on his stomach,
a finger to his lips and blows —
he can do a Louis like nobody else.
Turn,   to the Golden Oldies.
Sometimes, he calls me his favorite Supreme
or his one and only Apollo showgirl.

With the switch of a dial, we move in unison.
In the infinite dark, our flickering stations   *turn.*

Cinéma Vérité

—inspired by a 1968 photo in which a power worker
is electrocuted while strapped atop a pole

I. *The Arthouse*

It has nothing to do with desire
although the act of pushing air
from one set of lungs to another
suggests an intimacy between people.

They weren't supposed to meet;
they were always meant to be.
I watch each man on the street
the way dust swirls in the light —

the focus of gold endorphins.
The premise: two lovers in danger.

II. *The American Epic*

If anything, it starts with lust.
She watches from the porch.
He does his best to scale the pole.
She sweeps her hair, auburn and damp,

over one shoulder. She enjoys his arms,
they flex when the leather belt catches
and slaps the pole. He wants to wink
from under his hat. A print of tulips

covers her dress, petals and stems
in complete disarray. There's lipstick
on her teeth. Such details from so far away,
but it's like that sometimes.

He sweats continents down his back,
dark shapes rounding the shoulders,
narrow pike along the spine. She loves the image
so much, he's disconnected: two biceps and an arched back.

Up among the elms, the tools from his belt
shine diamonds. This charms her in some childish way.
His lean body out in the clouds. The sky numb blue
like her husband's eyes. He's near the top—

where the overhead lines are reported all dead.
He nods, she nods, a whiff of perfume floats up to him.
Soft, like her wide rear end. She is wonderfully exotic
among Fords and Buicks. He watches her sit on the stoop

and smooth her skirt before the livewire finds him,
changing the seconds between thinking *I want* and *I don't*
and *I want*. He dangles unconscious
to the rocking of her breasts. As she runs,

the fury of the tulips explodes into air.

III. *On the Cutting Room Floor*

For once there are no calls, no letters, just sun driving neighbors onto porches. 1968: heat like a long whistle, dry leaves scratching the curb, flip-flops sticking to swollen feet, the soft thump of plums falling to grass. It was a graveyard without bodies, each man arriving in the form of a letter. But some days, no one dies. I wish my father were here, Sam's father too. It could happen—at any moment. Mom screams when the worker's legs collapse and he hangs from a strap, bent at the knees like a purse emptied out of all its belongings. His hardhat cracks on the concrete. Mom races toward the street. Another man belts the pole in a frantic game of vertical leapfrog. *He knows how a charge can blaze through a body—leave holes where the electricity burns out.* He steadies his friend, cradles the head from hanging, places his mouth over the listless mouth and breathes sour air into the lungs. It's the slowest kiss that was never a kiss that I've ever seen. Mom's fingers brush over her lips, she blushes a necklace of welts. Pink flares along her cleavage and we both want this: to be kissed like that, to be jolted out and coaxed back. To stop and live again.

Father as Jellyfish

My son shivers in the babble of dreams.
　　For now, he only knows a few things:

rough beard, blankets and breasts. He grips
　　the world in his hands. Soon enough,

he'll spend words the way the nouveaux riches
　　burn money—with haste and an impracticality

for fashion. The jargon of the schoolyard, *snapcracklepop!*
　　Bling in the mouth, meaning askew.

Later, he'll strike pose after endless pose:
　　insecurity, pride and lust. His door will shut.

He'll figure if he's like most men:
　　average penis, thin arms, a basic understanding of math.

Will he work? Be an intellectual?
　　Will he break the earth with those soft hands?

But tonight, behind the bars of his crib,
　　he is a prince in the kingdom of rhymes.

From under the sea, he sees me:
　　hovering head and tentacles,

bloated and ripe with meaning.
　　As sleep descends, I arrange myself

floating near the shore of his life
　　like stars, like hurdles, like gravity.

Stingers in place, I wait.

Puberty in a Jar

In summer, we waste days
thinking of our hands
and what we can snag
in jars. Tired of spiders

and crickets and such,
we settle on salamanders.
We are specimen collectors,
scientists in shorts.

> *One wide, one tall.*
> *One brave, one small.*
> *Two friends, two boys.*
> *Two jars poised.*

The "Land of the Lost"
lay behind the row houses.
Downhill to the stream
through the weeds and the rot.

We disturb stones
on the bottom of the creek.
Clouds of sand and silt
waft out—dirty thoughts

underwater. Salamanders,
slick and dark as twigs,
quickly skim
the surface. We watch

for twisting blades of grass,
for pebbles that shift,
and shadows that aren't.
A hunting we will go.

"Be on the lookout," he shouts,
"Hold your jar ready
to snap the lid shut!"
The shade of the willow

covers us in ovals.
Light shimmies in cracks
along the water. His desire,
haphazard and sweet,

hangs in the air like musk,
clings to the rocks like mold.
"Get it!" I yell.
A narrow black tongue

shoots over his foot.
He smacks his jar underwater.
The creek and I
are sucked inside.

     Like Alice, like Dorothy—
     the world takes a spin.
     Sit and spin! Sit and spin!
     The critters all shout.

Glass breaks against the rocks.
Held in the sun, his hand
is dazzling covered in bits
of shards and mud. Blood

streaks through the creek
the color of cherries,
a lustful blush
that soon disappears.

Something Wicked

—Cincinnati, Ohio, 1979

The dead have followed from Korea.
    The moon and the branches

hang in the light like corpses.
    Duplicitous wind storms the yard;

the leaves and husks of insects shudder.
    Sheathed in curtains, covered in poppies—

orange and gold—her back is embroidered flame.
    There is no finer stitch than this:

marriage: always counting the details left,
    always waiting on the marbled foot.

The Nurse & the Lights

A heavyset nurse bends over
my father who on his belly
looks nothing like a baby.

She gently swabs
his rear end clean.
Snow falls

in the distant window.
It's near the holidays.
Her socks remind me.

Green holly & red berries
adorn her thick ankles.
Father's skin up in rows

from under her rag.
Not a hair out of place,
she smiles this look

of benevolence. It's Christmas,
& the workers in the heart
of the city are sweeping

debris from the streets
where they'll string white lights
around lampposts, around their monuments.

Peeping Toms

We crouch down, propped on fingertips,
and peer through the basement window.

It's amazing how light spreads in the dark
and the eyes adjust so that ideas become shapes

and the shapes become motions
like those in a cartoon flipbook.

My tallest cousin Richard,
whose nickname is "Shorty,"

elbows my darkest cousin, Casey,
whose nickname is "Blacky."

They call me "Grimace"
after the amorphous purple blob

from McDonaldland. Through the glass,
her skin is the color of parchment,

the light flickers along her spine.
Her flabby buttocks dimple

when she steps out of cotton panties.
The lightheaded gulf of embarrassment

warms my chubby cheeks and thighs.
She unhooks her bra and there they are:

the bike-tire cap of her nipples.
Shorty knew the words—pussy, snatch, and cunt.

We had all seen the clit with the staple
and the breasts with the tasteful blur but this—!

We leap over multiple hedges
and fumble through several backyards.

Her body refuses the terms,
the slang-by-number words,

we try to assign her body.

Burning Down Suburbia

—an Ode to Bob Ross

When I was younger, I watched the world blend
    on PBS. The painter with the *Jewfro* hypnotized me.

With a thumb hooked through the palette,
    he painted forward from the base coat

like a god might use a blueprint.
    Behind the image is always the word:

light. On top came tiny crisscross strokes
    of phthalo blue. A rapturous pinwheel of words

unveiled sky. Two sharp strokes of titanium white
    slashed with gray from the master's knife

became wings, gulls taking flight. I begged for nothing
    but paints that summer. Already equipped with an afro,

I sat before the paper and the cakes of color
    and tried to figure out the path to cerulean,

the wrist twist to evergreens and the motion
    for clouds. The oversaturated paper dried and cracked

with the fine lines of lightning. The worlds he reproduced
    might as well have been Asgard or Olympus.

How I longed for a visit. Might he come
    armed with a fan brush and dressed in a button down?

To be soothed by his voice and taken,
    lured from the dining-room table and shown

the suburb's majesty. Look son, he might say,
    at the pile of autumn leaves, the shade

on that forest-green trash bag. Using his two-inch brush
    he'd blend the prefab homes on the hill

until they seemed mysterious, folded hues
    of Prussian blue, Van Dyke brown, and a blaze of alizarin crimson.

Portrait of My Father as a Young Black Man

—Cincinnati, Ohio, 1987

Rage is the language of men,
    layers of particulates fused.

    Rage is the wine
        father pours to the ground

        for men whose time has passed. Rage
        is gripped in the hands

    like the neck of a broom held tight. Rage
gets stuck in the throat, suppressed.

Rage is a promise kept.

The Nuclear Family

—Cincinnati, Ohio, 1988

Dad calls from a pay phone next to a bus stop. A bus comes to a screeching halt and the doors slap open. It lets out a wheeze of passengers like Cronus passing Olympians. The warm air changes the very texture of their skin. Dad's on his way to see the baby's mama and wants to bring her by the laundromat. There's a pause as the bus doors suck closed. He says, don't look at her arms. She's got track marks and doesn't like people staring at her arms. I envision the scar as a long, candied worm.

— — —

Once, he brought a tall mulatto to his mother's house. He was fresh out of prison and staying in the basement on Orchard Lane. He wanted her to have some homemade rolls and she clacked around the kitchen in five-inch heels, offering to help. She pulled her long, *good hair* back over one shoulder as she cracked the lid of pot after steaming pot. This did not endear her to my grandmother. Carissa looked like a movie star or a singer, some type of chanteuse. They played spades after dinner and I sat under the table looking at all the shoes: Granny's rosebud embroidered slippers, Dad's slip-on dress shoes, and Aunt Pam's regulated, uniform, nurse shoes. Besides her heels, red, Carissa wore a golden anklet. I thought, she must have a treasure hidden somewhere.

— — —

Dad calls from a pay phone at the corner to say they're at the corner. When the bells on the front door jingle, I stiffen. She has the baby in her arms wrapped in a Winnie-the-Pooh blanket. I can't see his face and she's wearing a long-sleeve tee in the middle of summer. Shirley's Laundromat is only half full because most of the college kids have gone home to places like New Hampshire or Maine. Back then, I thought all college kids came from places like New Hampshire or Maine. Dad's arm is wrapped around her shoulders and she sticks out a blanched hand to shake. She eyes the candy on the counter and I say, have a Snickers or a Whatchamacallit. She says thanks and rips the wrapper open with her teeth. Dad says, this is your new brother. The fuzz on his head is like the new hair growing on the sides of my hands which have become long and unfamiliar. A guy with a tattoo needs help with his washer. He comes to the counter and the family backs away. Dad waves, I'll see you at home. The family leaves and the yellow laundromat seems smaller and dingier. The floor tile is warped and cracked. Spin cycles begin their noisy rotation. I make change for a dollar and sell another box of detergent. The scent of Bounce wafts down from the dryers and I read the small boxes behind the counter: *New and Improved, Longer Lasting, Freshness from Start to Finish.*

The Savages in the Suburbs

—Cincinnati blizzard, 1978

After school, mom asks, *What you learn today?* Meaning, *What new word did you learn today?* She pushes a sheet of paper across the table and slaps down a pen beside it. This is not a casual inquiry: what I learn, *she learns*, and I take my time with each letter.

— — —

Like anticipating signals from space, we wait for the words *Taylor Elementary: Closed* to scroll across the bottom of the screen—but it never happens. It's dark and my mother sighs; dad's at work. She curses in a mixture of Korean and English and stomps off to find pink moonboots. Zipping me up to the chin and wrapping my scarf like seaweed, she motions for me to jump on, piggyback style.

The street is lined with odd submarines, cars afloat in snow. It's like the time I fiddled with the hole in my stuffed Rin Tin Tin, the World's Most Famous Dog, and his innards fell out all fluffy and white. Each car is frosted with seven-inch layers on top. My mom, in the live-action version of *Frogger*, navigates the long, white dashes. Side to side and down the middle, not much chance of getting run over. Yards away, curtains part and Adam's mom looks out in shock. Adam waves, but Mrs. Seegler cinches her bathrobe tight. *It's 1978 for God's sake.* Blinds are cracked and shades snap up as the neighbors follow us like klieg lights.

Insomniacs

Pop told me a story once:
men with guns were after him
and a whore in a high-speed car chase.
Fidel! she screamed, Fidel because
that's what friends called him
in the neighborhood. It was the eighties
and he had this thing for Castro.
She yelled as he pushed her
wild yellow mop below the dashboard.
Bullets sprayed the windshield
and he swerved into the night
around blocks he knew better
than anyone: Vine, McMillan, Race.

And I wait for him to cross
the threshold of that world
into the world in which I live:
pale blue, stuck in the ash
of late-night TV. I watch
reruns of cop shows. In each,
my father is the crook and
I am the law that cuffs him.
Here in the morning, before
light becomes an issue, before
people get ready for work.

Price Check

At the A&P, angry men with matted hair
        and fistfuls of change drop their coins

in front of the register. They pile cans
        of potted meat on the belt and reluctantly wait

as the cashier shuffle-counts pennies
        into the palm of his hand. *Stupid college boy.*

There's a shelter next door that leans to the right
        like a drunk with cracked white shutters

and spray-painted columns tagged with gang signs.
        An apocalyptic Tara in the heart of Midtown.

The smell of the patrons lingers all day:
        KOOLs, sex and damp T-shirts. A woman with too much rouge

digs through an old purse. Her wig is slanted
        and she needs two dimes. Or four nickels.

A Victorian gone awry. Something about the intensity,
        the absolute belief that two small coins

will appear, reminds the cashier of his mother —
        the day the odd car pulled up to the lawn.

He's seven and she's been gone for months.
        She's freshly scrubbed and her face is blanched.

His father tips the driver and his mother
        searches a small, clear bag with a comb, Vaseline,

and countless tin wrappers folded like birds
      for one stick of gum. She hands it to him

like it's her only possession and he counts it
      as if it's all that he needs.

Three Ways to Scat about a Leg & a Father

1

If I could scat about the moon hung low
over the river like an ornament
or a sentimental piece of rock,

what would I say? Something memorable,
something more than a scoobie-de-doo.
Tonight, the fog rolls like slow music,

the moon is a monster under sheets.

The band of guardian angels
hanging outside the window jive,
"Man, that cat is square."

They're only stars I tell myself,
irked at how they see me,
bare-ass behind glass —

a stuffed dove
in the glare
of starlight.

2

Maybe the moon is an RSVP
for the utmost swank occasion.

The crickets are bit players
in this orchestra pit.

There are the feverish sounds
of stroking legs of awkward pity.

The stars are guests & linger,
small bright scabs in the sky.

3

He's drunk out there
in the mist between the hills
     playing trumpet without his prosthesis.
     With sores that shine like sequins, *the body,* he riffs

        is like a neon sign: *sometimes on*
                  & sometimes off.

Asylum

A woman moved is like a fountain troubled,
Muddy, ill-seeming, thick, bereft of beauty;
And while it is so, none so dry or thirsty
Will deign to sip or touch one drop of it.
                    —Katherina, Shakespeare's *The Taming of the Shrew*

At the end of the play, the cast collects itself
and the principals make speeches of uncanny humility.
At the end of her life, mother collects her knives,
places them in her pocketbook along with spearmint gum.

    Of course, these will be confiscated, the knives.
    She takes a few novels for the ride, thick ones
    that will last the whole time. She likes *Shogun*
    and *The Godfather*, men with vices and violent lives.

She packs her pink-and-green curling iron
which she no longer uses but remembers
how the heat burned her scalp before the slightest
indescribable pleasure. The car is waiting.

    She looks at the boy and pushes
    with all her might the rock up the hill
    to recognize him, to stay in the moment,
    to silence the wind that carries her name

and the men who hide behind trees. This boy
                    she notes for a second—the slightest,
                                    indescribable pleasure.

Agnostic Front

I believe the spine was stolen
    right out of my father's back.

Slumped at the kitchen table,
    he doesn't move. Beyond the window,

light pierces the clouds,
    inspires all matter to burst.

Father had a way with explosions.
    The noon sun's breaking and entering

his head—smashing the temple
    and storming his heart. The dark organ stops.

Arteries close for grief. Love leaves the barest
    bones of a thought: clouds evaporate.

How the spit pools and falls to the tile.

The Widower

The real test of love happens afterward,
the spin cycle over, plates rinsed,
the dish towel threaded through the door.
It happens when you've picked his best suit,
shined his shoes and had the right rouge
applied—so it seems he's aged
without any kind of pock or blemish.
Belief in your own mythology—
the apartments, the toasters, and the mixers.
Mismatched silverware and such.
Will it lead a man back? Will he come
when all the roads lay open?
Will he settle for the dusty light that shines
through all those kitchen windows?

Death Is a One-Night Stand

A poor boy promised me a textbook view
    of the stars. No snaking city lights
        from a crown of downtown buildings,

Medusa-like in their paralyzing beauty.
    He drives the dark highway
        and I hold him to his word, he turns

onto a roughly paved hillside.
    Stiff black trunks and treetops wave
        good-bye from the roadside. Visions of policemen

in orange reflective vests
    pulled by search dogs for a scent,
        a scrap of cloth, follow me into the field.

He places a hand on the dip of my back
    to guide me, like Hades, into his world.

Balanchine's *Prodigal Son*

—for Calvin Shawn Landers, Dance Theater of Harlem

On his first night in Manhattan, he dons
an acid-washed jean jacket, turns up the collar,
and stands on the 1/9 train even though
there are more than enough seats. White tank top,
jeans cuffed at the bottom, and combat boots.
Lightly, he treads the pavement pocked
with blackened gum like stage marks.
Through the white-tile tunnel and up the steps
onto 42nd Street, he emerges into radiance.
If this were a Broadway play,
his imperious grace would assume
first position on the corner, maybe
a *pas de bourrée couru* through the crosswalk,
ending with a *Grand Jeté* in front of an American flag
composed entirely of neon lights. Could it begin
any other way? The ticker of the stock exchange
relays the world's worth and Adonis's billboard,
abs cut in shadows and digitally retouched crotch,
hangs above him. Like so many that fall
to the elixir of lights of this corporate-
sponsored space station, he sees the promise
inherent in the landscape, the technological address
of desire. The gravity of the Midwest behind him,
the weightlessness of youth in his gate,
he takes a small *pas de chat* for mankind.

Glorious Hole

In a place without light, we have our sex.
The cool harbor of bathroom floors,
the cerebral smell of tile. I wait
with mouth open, adjacent to the rim,
for fluid perfect and unclear. I wait
for a place where cells won't die
in the mouth but leap off the tongue—
wise and physical like gods.

Next to Him

It's not about the sex, really, it's not
the ache of the bruised nipple or the burn
left by his two-day-old beard in the crook
of my neck where the pulse is taken, it's
his breathing when asleep that draws me near.
When I was seventeen, I'd check beside me,
hope I hadn't rolled and squashed flat
my one-year-old brother. His sigh on my ear,
the rise and fall of air beneath his ribs,
was a miracle to me. The nightly
surprise of what I saw under the bulb's
dim glow: I saw the small heart beating
like wings unfolding in the body. Here,
with this man, ideas of flight return.

The Green Bowls

My lover bought me green bowls. I had none.
Green or otherwise. I served dessert on
saucers and never had more than one guest.
Later, he brought two irregular spoons.
Long, with a tiny scoop. He didn't know
these were properly used to stir iced tea.
I didn't mind. We sat on my futon
waving the wands, eating small bits of pie.
The pie seems to last much longer. When he
unwrapped two plates, the same shade as the bowls,
I knew I was in love but would have to
cook. We stood over the kitchen counter
as if taken by surprise. Centered in sheets
of newsprint lay not ordinary plates,
but a new shape entering our lives.

Small Mausoleums

If you know something, *Call Jan*
                        is written in the clearest cursive

with perfectly looped l's
                        and a's that seem wide open.

His image, his tiny mouth
                        is taped to a bus shelter,

all four corners secured
                        so he won't blow away

or come undone. He hangs
                        like a clipping—an APT 4 RENT

or a Futon 4 Sale. The bottom
                        slashed into tabs that are easily ripped

if you know something. *Call Jan*
                        is written in the clearest cursive

with perfectly looped l's
                        and a's that seem wide open.

Midlife Crisis in Boots

He winces at the cruelty but keeps
his eyes fixed on the thick twisting neck

      wider than a man's torso. He taps my wrist,
      aims for a look or a nod to confirm

our distance from this, but I refuse
to see beyond the fairground:

      the aluminum benches, the dirt arena,
      ground shells of peanuts beneath boots.

It's all so matter of fact—
the lasso's anticipatory twirl,

      the instant snapback of the calf's neck.
      He stares as if to signal *enough*.

But secretly, as the calf is roped
and the rope pulled tight, the lover

      is envious: the cowboy leaps from his horse,
        suspended midair—violent and capable

                        of anything.

The Messenger

All the myths are different: his mother
wears light thrown off from the fireplace
like jewelry. She rubs the bones of his foot
and traces the arch back to a story
in which his granddad is bedridden.
He's coughing, hacking up phlegm into cups
his daughters empty. This was our duty,
his mother says and we carried those cups
not spilling a single drop because we thought
the more we emptied out, the less fluid
in his lungs. This was our bright idea
of curing his sickness. Mama was in a trance
like the old folks in church and just like the old folks

she burst from her seat, a cloud of hair
puffed dust gray. She pleaded with the spirits.
Have mercy, she demanded. I stared into the bulb,
bare and white, until I mistook spots
for God's glory. I knew Jean not only saw
the same thing, marble-sized pulsing flashes,
but heard the music too. Over papa's coughing
and mama's ranting, the whippoorwill's call.
Mama was not talking to God but a bird
that had landed on her roof. Nuts, Jean said,
gone nuts. We trailed her blue slippers
to the attic window and it slid up with a moan.
We watched her beat the black-tarred roof
until her hands swelled but that bird remained unmoved.

The Pear Tree

We plan for the storm by severing the limbs

of a tree so close its branches covet

our house. Really, it's my lover,

the practical one, who eyes the danger.

He stalks up the ladder with the saw,

places the teeth against the bark and grunts

before his bicep finds its rhythm. His footing

worries me, the quivering calf

framed by the kitchen window.

Inside, I entertain friends: fill a teapot

and arrange some snacks. Radha says,

she likes the place but all I hear

is the preaching wind, testimony of the clamoring leaves.

Framed by the kitchen window,

blossoms—suicidal brides plummeting.

"Mommy," her small boy asks, "Why is that tree crying?"

Type 2

When I wake, this is what I tell myself:
    I belong to this, to all the ghosts present

in the DNA. Diabetes,
    an ancient Greek consort, sweeps through the halls

of my body. It seems the proper gift
    from my father, memory locked down in the cells

of my bladder. Frequent urination
    is a hard nag to beat. My body

is my father's complaint. He rings at two
    in the morning. A piss in the pot, a shot

in the dark. He's never too far away.

Night Sweats

—after Lucille Clifton

You sleep as I imagine
a superhero flies:
one arm straight
and one leg cocked,
skimming the froth
of cumulonimbus.

Beads of rain
break against your skin
speeding home.

As if Metropolis
wasn't enough,
the subconscious plunders
to be remembered.

Again, you are otherworldly:
sleeping in another tongue.
When you awake,
you spiral back and seem
so utterly fragile. Your name
should have been Clark.

In Need of Subtitles

Because I can never say anything
    plainly. Because I always stutter
        politely. Because there's always the chatter

        before the kiss, I want him to know—
I'll wait. Like the dames in old MGM films
wrapped in scarves and wisps

of cigarette smoke. He turns,
    smiles and waves, boards the plane. It's all
        there in his wrist, the eagerness to go.

        As the plane turns to make its ascent,
    my fingers remember the strings,
holding the pick in one hand,

the idea of strumming in my head.
    How to make the two connect
        as he rumbles away, my cargo as much

        as the plane's. *He moves my wrist,*
    positions my finger with the pick,
presses down on the nail determining the note.

I think he has a seat by the window.
    Shadow in a body that hovers.
        Face pressed to the glass

        and kissing my ass good-bye. Good riddance.
    He moves my wrist up and down again.
and laughs. Enough about guitars, I say.

His forearm brushes my fingers or is it
my fingers that brush his forearm. No one ever imagines
the tendons as soft but that's the skin I suppose.

What will he play without me?

Rapture

Prologue

When I could identify longing,
unravel it from melancholy
or a predetermined kind of ache, I knew
I'd prefer an older man's belly
to the flat abdomen and sharp hip bones
of the young. This desire, mostly tactile,
started as a child—scooping the dirt
and building the mound to zip a car over—
sailing into a pyramid of pop cans.
I'd like to say much has changed since then,
but I knead my lover's stomach
in the same exacting motion, pressing down
for firmness as he waves the flag, a sign—
gentlemen, please start your engines.

I. *Twenty-One*

I tuck the sheet under both arms, tidying
after lust. I hear an arch of urine
fizzing in the bowl. Is this what father meant
    when he stood and explained, *Be careful?*
    Before leaving, he made toast and eggs over easy.
    A meal to coat the stomach. Did he know
        about the men taking laps around the bar
        until finding a spot to eye a boy,
        pare him down, undo his clothes, molecule
            by molecule, as if wearing X-ray specs
            found only in the backs of comic books?
        He must've known about the grope and the rub down,
            the mashed mouths, the need to join, the legs
            pinned like insect wings to a headboard.
        He must have known the odds of failure, the odds
            of being twenty-one. How darkness is
            more of a presence than desire, how
            the absence of a lover is tedious.
                How the flush of a toilet serves as warning:
                more emptiness to come.

II. *The Tunnel*

Past velvet ropes like arteries—
    jungle drums, a Teutonic march, a twitch he feels
        in his thumbs. Automatic bleats, the Stygian darkness,

the whine of sirens blares.
    Techno-lightning and the frozen repose—
        slick, bare backs, raw nerves exposed. Safe,

in the anonymity of the warehouse.
    Hundreds of workers never shuffled like this.
        Pulse in the wrist, the neck, the hips. He's skinned

like an apple, the continuous peel. Fever
    like a virus handclaps its way down—
        man after man after man.

III. *Ursa Major*

He pauses before entering, a part of him
    still recognizes fear, the panic
before sex. He smiles: *you'll be okay.* He bears down
    and I lose sight of him. I cannot
interpret this gravity, imagination
    replaced—the steady suck and release.
He quakes like a bear tearing down the tundra
    splaying bits of snow into the air.

IV. *Untitled*

The engine of his car turns over. Beads of dew
slide down the hood as he turns out the gravel drive.
In bed, long legs revel in the extra space
of having an additional side. To calculate
love's aftermath, one sees the world through a scrim.
         There's proof of God in light like this
                and the constant clink of the ceiling fan
                       sounds like a call to prayer.

V. *I'd Rather Be Eating*

Orchestrated better than the finest waiters,
ice cubes clink in the kitchen. I unravel
the knot, let the steam out, and arrange

the greasy cartons in the center. The TV
winks like candlelight and my love
holds two plastic cups: Diet Coke and 7Up.

I uncap the duck sauce, the fish sauce and place
each dip on the side of us. He moves
for the noodles white and slick with a forkful

of pork and mint. I sip a bit of broth
and slip a sock off. He plunks a roll
wrapped tight like a penis into the thick plum mud.

VI. *Civil Union*

No line will ever begin,
"As I lovingly look at my sleeping wife . . ."

At best, the winter keeps us mummified,
    swathed in blankets and sheets. I look over
at my partner — because he snores —
    and I imagine us as soldiers
locked down in a trench under the tarp
    of a foreign night. Who else is there to consider
when the lights click off and there's nothing left
    but right-wing, warfare metaphors? His snoring
as shrapnel, our farting as mutual,
    biological terror, this continued
breathing as a sign of dual surrender.

VII. *Rapture*

The gray skin of our legs plumes forth like smoke.
We braid those limbs and settle
into the milk-blue light. Cast
before one another, blemishes apparent,
slim thatches of grass poking through islands
of snow. We hold in place and refuse to cum:
an old LP, a needle tracing static,
a record ready to drop.

      Walnuts smack on the roof.

          A cardinal shakes on the line.

               And still, we refuse to yield

                    back into being singular.

Notes

The first few lines in "Father & Son by Window" are inspired by Dinah Washington crooning "Soft Winds."

The poem "Neckbone" is for Reetika Vazirani.

"Cinéma Vérité" is inspired by Sheryle and John Leekley's collection *Moments: The Pulitzer Prize Photographs*, in particular, the description of Rocco Morabito's 1968 photograph, *Kiss of Life:*

> The fact is, all the lines are dead—except one. That single live wire finds Champion . . . the life is virtually jolted out of him. He is left dangling upside down, blue, and unconscious. His buddies know in an instant: How the charge can blaze right through a body, leaving holes where the electricity burns out. How there is so little time.

"Father as Jellyfish" is for Jason Graham.

"Small Mausoleums" is a poem about the days following 9/11. Flyers were posted all over Manhattan for missing loved ones. Candles were burned on the corners and sidewalks were covered in wax. Bus shelters were graveyards.

"The Pear Tree" is for Reetika Vazirani and her son, Jehan, as told by Lailee Mendelson.

Acknowledgments

Acknowledgment and thanks to the editors and staff of the following publications in which versions of these poems first appeared:

African American Review (Balanchine's *Prodigal Son,* The Nuclear Family)
Black Warrior Review (His Face Is as Far Away as the Light)
Bloom (Death Is a One-Night Stand)
Brilliant Corners (Three Ways to Scat about a Leg & a Father)
Calalloo (Father & Son by Window)
Cavalier Literary Couture (Cinéma Vérité)
Chicago Quarterly Review (Bedtime Story #1, Midlife Crisis in Boots)
Common Ground Review (Agnostic Front, Asylum, Something Wicked)
Estuary (Portrait of My Father as a Young Black Man, Insomniacs, In Need of Subtitles, Type 2)
The Evergreen Review (The Savages in the Suburbs)
Gargoyle (Burning Down Suburbia, Night Sweats)
The Greensboro Review (Yellow Apples)
Ozone Park Journal (Neckbone)
Rearview Quarterly (The Messenger)
River Oak Review (Price Check, Smoke & Mirrors)
Salamander (The Pear Tree, Winter Anesthesia)
Shenandoah (The Green Bowls, Next to Him)
Slipstream (Glorious Hole, Peeping Toms)
The Southern Review (Father as Jellyfish, The Nurse & the Lights)
Valparaiso Poetry Review (The Widower)
Willow Springs (How to Move)

First and foremost, thank you to Tracy K. Smith for selecting this manuscript and hearing the voices within it. Because I am a teacher, I'd like to thank my teachers: Mary Hennigan, Carol Wuebbling, Henri Cole, Wayne Dodd, Tom Andrews, Rita Dove, Gregory Orr, and Charles Wright. Thanks also to the Academy of American Poets, the Community of Writers at Squaw Valley, the poets in the University of Virginia's graduate workshop (1995–1997), and everyone at Graywolf Press. Thank you to Andy Jones for bringing so much joy into my life. Thanks to Tracy Wilking and Ruth Dickey whose encouragement and support made this work possible. Finally, love to my family, Michael + Lucy, for this wonderfully textured life.

SJOHNNA MCCRAY was born and raised in Cincinnati, Ohio. He was educated at Ohio University and received his MFA from the University of Virginia where he was a Hoyns Fellow. He has a master's degree in English Education from Teachers College, Columbia University. McCray was the winner of the AWP Intro Journal Award and Ohio University's Emerson Poetry Prize. His work has appeared in numerous journals including the *Southern Review, Chicago Quarterly Review,* and *Shenandoah.* He lives and teaches in Savannah, Georgia.

The text of *Rapture* is set in Cochin. Book design by Rachel Holscher. Composition by Bookmobile Design and Publishing Services, Minneapolis, Minnesota. Manufactured by Versa Press on acid-free, 30 percent postconsumer wastepaper.